Warwickshire County Council

BED 10/15			

This item is to be returned or renewed before the latest date above. It may be borrowed for a further period if not in demand. **To renew your books:**

- **Phone the 24/7 Renewal Line 01926 499273 or**
- **Visit www.warwickshire.gov.uk/libraries**

Discover • Imagine • Learn • *with libraries*

 Warwickshire County Council

Working for Warwickshire

DISCARDED

KEITH PIRT COLOUR PORTFOLIO

WESTERN REGION

Keith R. Pirt

BOOK LAW PUBLICATIONS

This portrait of 'Dukedog' No.9021, at Portmadoc station in August 1958, is typical of the work produced by Keith Pirt during nearly fifty years of colour photography. Herein we present some more of his Western Region studies. BLP - W89.

First published in the United Kingdom by Book Law Publications 2006
382 Carlton Hill, Nottingham, NG4 1JA
Printed and bound by The Amadeus Press, Cleckheaton, West Yorkshire.

INTRODUCTION

This album of Keith Pirt's Western Region steam locomotive subjects illustrates a cross section of those locomotives still active on the region during the late 1950s and early 60s'. Not surprisingly a number of branch lines are observed when they were still doing business - just. The main line action covers a broad spectrum of the region from Sonning to Hatton to Dawlish, Rattery, Bodmin Road and of course the Cambrian lines. Locomotives are seen in shiny bright livery and in the filthy neglected state which became so commonplace towards the end. One thing all the views have in common though is sunshine, no matter what the season, the sun light was always there to lift the gloom. If you like lots of smoke and steam then this collection will suit you nicely.

A fair amount of allocation history is included within the captions and of course we include withdrawal dates and cut-up venues in many cases. It is this latter aspect of the 'potted' locomotive history which brings out a fact which is obviously pure coincidence but nevertheless thought provoking - most of the engines featured were scrapped by one company; J.Cashmore. The transparencies used in this album were chosen at random and it was only when the research for each caption was completed that the 'coincidence' was noted.

Anyway, enjoy these nostalgic recollections through the medium of KRP's colour photography.

David Allen, Book Law Publications, Nottingham.

Locomotives featured in this album:

1419	1424	1453	1470	1472	2232	2866	3200	3806
3834	4075	4081	4086	4104	4118	4125	4552	4559
4569	4587	4666	4919	4954	4967	4974	5007	5024
5060	5067	5080	5091	5183	5198	5311	5410	5515
5552	5557	5614	5957	5968	6008	6011	6019	6024
6138	6324	6604	6821	6867	6940	7002	7024	7027
7031	7800	7801	7810	7816	7819	7826	7827	7828
7913	7924	8106	9021	9765.				

St Blazey engine shed was responsible for the motive power which served Fowey and the branch lines therefrom. In July 1957 14XX No.1419 waits amidst the summer flowers at Fowey with the auto-train for Lostwithiel. Resident at St Blazey for all it's BR career, the four-coupled tank ended its days at Swindon works having been withdrawn at 83E in April 1961. It was cut up during the following August. Note that the train coach was one of the old wooden bodied variety. *BLP - W10.*

In the year when it was withdrawn, Collett 14XX 0-4-2T No.1472 is seen near Brimscombe on a Gloucester to Chalford branch Auto-train during April 1964. This engine had worked the Chalford branch since its transfer to Horton Road shed in Gloucester from Weymouth in March 1959. Up to being put into store at the former Midland Railway roundhouse at Gloucester Barnwood in October 1964, and then its condemnation a month later, No.1472 was amongst the last of its class still working though Nos.1442 and 1450 managed to outlast it by six months at Exmouth Junction shed. Considering their diminutive size, some of the engines in this class certainly managed to get around the old GWR system; in its BR existence alone, No.1472 worked at Carmarthen, Newton Abbot and Weymouth before ending up in Gloucester. By February 1965 it was resident in Cashmores Newport yard awaiting the cutters torch. *BLP - W13.*

A delightful scene near Golant Halt on the estuarine branch line between Lostwithiel and Fowey in June 1960. 14XX No.1419 is crossing a creek embankment with a midday Fowey bound service. Golant Halt was the only intermediate station on the branch north of Fowey and it survived to the cessation of passenger services on the branch in 1965 when Fowey also closed. A thriving china clay traffic has helped to keep this line open and the loading jetties alongside the river at Carne Point are still fed by this branch line which although closed between Fowey and St Blazey, is still accessible from the main line at Lostwithiel. *BLP - W85.*

Another little gem for the 14XX fans. Newton Abbot based No.1470 stands at Ashburton station dock with the branch auto-train in July 1957. Sporting a nice black livery, the 0-4-2T contrasts nicely with the red painted passenger stock. The Ashburton branch closed in 1958 but the section between the main line at Totnes and Buckfastleigh has been restored and now forms part of the Dart Valley Railway. Sadly, the part of the branch featured here could not be saved in time but we have the likes of pictures such as these to remind us of what a delightful part of England, complete with miniature gas holders, this line served. The 14XX remained at 83A until May 1961 when it transferred to Exeter shed for further auto-work on the branches radiating from Tiverton but sadly it did not outlive these branch lines and was withdrawn in October 1962 after being stored for some time beforehand. *BLP - W14.*

In April 1963 14XX No.1472 was employed on an afternoon service from Gloucester and is seen en route to Chalford shortly after departure from Brimscombe station and has now just passed the banking engine shed there. Besides the intermediate stations such as Stroud and Brimscombe, there were at least half a dozen halts on this route between Stonehouse and Chalford, some with platforms and shelters which, on first impression, would easily pass for a station rather than a mere halt. *BLP - W99.*

Yet another 14XX beauty. No.1453 enters Chalford station on an auto-train service from Gloucester in April 1963. Seven of these 0-4-2Ts ended their days at Gloucester working the last of the Chalford auto-trains up to the withdrawal of the service in 1964. After being put into storage at Gloucester Barnwood shed in October 1964, No.1453 was condemned during November and after a couple of months it was hauled north to Great Bridge for scrapping, the only one of the seven to make that particular journey. Most of it's BR service was completed at Weymouth shed although it spent short periods at Slough and Banbury before reaching Gloucester Horton Road in August 1962. Up to 1935 Chalford possessed an engine shed situated on the Up side of the line west of the station. This had been built in 1903 for a railmotor which stabled overnight but when they were withdrawn and replaced by locomotive hauled trains, the shed was demolished and a servicing point with water and coal facilities took its place. *BLP - W49.*

9

14XX No.1419 again in June 1960 alongside the estuary near Golant halt. One can readily appreciate why GWR modellers find these locomotives and their small trains so attractive. *BLP - W209.*

To finish off our sequence of 14XX 0-4-2Ts, we present this view of No.1424 strolling along the main line through the Golden Valley with a Chalford service on a superb day in April 1963. Will the 'Pacer' and 'Sprinter' diesel units bring the same nostalgic recollections in years to come? *BLP - W121.*

Aberystwyth engine shed, July 1963. Visible on the yard are three 'Manors', one 32XX, two 8XXXX BR Standard tanks and one of the 82XXX variety. The shed in view dated from 1938 when the original Cambrian Railway shed, part of which dated to the A&WCR in 1864, was replaced by this two-road brick built structure. Re-gauged in 1965, this particular shed is now part of the Vale of Rheidol narrow gauge complex. The depot site at Aberystwyth also had another interesting shed on the site which was erected by the Manchester & Milford Railway at an unknown date. A one road dead-end type building, it was apparently utilised as a repair shop by the GWR after 1923 but was demolished when yard improvements took place in the 1930s. From this angle, that shed would have been between the elevated coal stage and the engine shed. Aberystwyth motive power depot closed to standard gauge steam locomotives in April 1965 and the remaining allocation was transferred to Machynlleth. *BLP - W138.*

'Manors' 7827 LYDHAM MANOR, 7828 ODNEY MANOR, 7801 ANTHONY MANOR and BR Standard Cl.3 No.82005 bask in the sun outside Machynlleth engine shed in July 1963. Resident No.7827, with 7828 behind, were both being prepared for Royal Train duty and as can be seen are immaculate. Shrewsbury based No.7801 is, on the other hand, just clean. The shed here was established by the Newtown & Machynlleth Railway in 1863 when this three road building was erected. The following year that company was absorbed by the Cambrian Railway who in turn added a two road extension to the northern end of the shed. The facilities were basic with a manual coal stage and turntable and things remained much the same until the depot closed to steam in December 1966. By then the 'namers' were all gone and BR Standard tanks became the last steam residents. The two 4-6-0s involved with Royal Train duties ended up preserved whilst 7801 was sold for scrap in early 1966. *BLP - W172.*

A nice study of 'Dukedog' No.9021 resting at Portmadoc shed in August 1958. The Machynlleth based 4-4-0 was eking out its last months of life before withdrawal in the coming November. It was cut up at Swindon during the following February. The year 1957 was a particularly bad one for this twenty-nine strong class when fourteen of the twenty-one survivors were condemned. Most of them had been in storage throughout that year, their work given over to the new BR Standard classes which were by then infiltrating the Cambrian lines. Although No.9021 had been in store during much of 1957 it was resurrected and put to work for another year. The ancestry of the 'Dukedog' class, though nominally 1930s rebuilds, goes back to the 1890s 'Duke of Cornwall' class and the early 1900s 'Bulldog' class. The boilers of the rebuilds were provided by the 'Dukes' whilst the 'Bulldogs' supplied the frames - hence the name 'Dukedog'. So, in essence, No.9021 was older than the shed that occasionally housed it. The two road, brick built, dead-ended structure at Portmadoc, a portion of which can be seen on the right, dated from 1907 and was built by the Cambrian Railway to replace an earlier one-road structure on the same site. The facilities at the later shed were somewhat basic and the depot was closed by British Railways in August 1963. *BLP - W69.*

Brimscombe engine shed was home for the banking engines used on Sapperton bank on the line towards Kemble. In this April 1963 view the resident 'bankers' were two 41XX class 2-6-2Ts, the first of which was No.4104 with 4100 behind. Horton Road shed provided the engines, on a weekly basis and the change round occurred to enable washing out and routine maintenance to be carried out a the parent shed in Gloucester. The engine shed at Brimscombe dated from 1845 and was erected simply to house the engines employed banking goods trains, and the occasional passenger train to the summit situated between two tunnels. The shed in view is the original brick building with a later stone built extension erected to carry the substantial water tank, site restrictions precluded using any other location. The shed was closed at the end of October 1963 when steam banking was abolished on Sapperton. What of the 'Prairie' tanks? No.4100 worked at 85B until November 1965 and was then sold for scrap to Buttigiegs in Newport. No.4104 had succumbed earlier in May 1964 and within weeks of withdrawal had joined many other BR steam locomotives at Cashmores yard in Newport. *BLP - W100.*

Getting a helping hand from an unseen banker on Rattery bank, St Philips Marsh 'Grange' No.6867 PETERSTON GRANGE plods westward with a Down freight in July 1957. This 4-6-0 had been a Bristol engine since at least 1950 but in December 1957 it transferred to Laira but only for three months after which it returned north and went as far as Stafford Road shed. Again, the engine got itchy feet after less than three months and was off to Pontypool Road where it settled down until June 1963 when it reallocated to Neath. Exactly a year later, its final transfer took it to Llanelly but fortune dictated that suitable work, even for a useful mixed traffic type, was thin on the ground and in August the inevitable took place - No.6867 was condemned. By the end of the year it was resident in the Bridgend scrapyard of Birds Commercial Motors. *BLP - W63.*

Tyseley based 'Hall' No.4954 PLAISH HALL creates a curving steam and smoke exhaust as it climbs Hatton bank with this long freight in November 1961. These versatile locomotives were equally at home hauling goods or passenger traffic. No.4954 had certainly 'done the rounds' during its BR career being allocated, in chronological order, to Bristol Bath Road, Plymouth Laira, Exeter, Newton Abbot, Didcot, Oxford, Wolverhampton Stafford Road, Tyseley and finally Oxley. Withdrawn in November 1964, it was taken into Cashmores Great Bridge yard before that year was out. *BLP - W268.*

With its tender full, Severn Tunnel Junction's 28XX class 2-8-0 No.3806 returns home through Sonning cutting with a train of empty mineral wagons in April 1962. Looking the part for the period, the locomotive is somewhat filthy and was more than likely to stay that way until withdrawal at its then new home, Banbury shed, in December 1963. Much of its life, indeed until it's July 1962 transfer to Banbury, was spent at two South Wales depots - Ebbw Junction and Severn Tunnel Junction. It ended up being scrapped by J.Cashmore at their Great Bridge yard. *BLP - W96.*

28XX No.3834, of Newton Abbot shed, also has charge of a train of empty mineral wagons in July 1957. The location is Dawlish and the 2-8-0 is taking advantage of the slight lull in the early morning traffic as it makes its way north towards the South Wales coalfield which at that time could boast to having over one hundred and thirty working collieries. How far the 2-8-0 would have taken this particular train is unknown to the writer but Taunton would seem as good a place as any where a similar train, but loaded, would be waiting in the yards there for transit to the West Country. Formerly at Exeter, No.3834 moved to Newton Abbot in September 1950 for a nine year residency. In November 1959 it transferred to Llanelly and then, some nine months later it moved to Severn Tunnel Junction. Southall was its next shed but not until November 1962 did it go there. Finally, it was allocated to Taunton in June 1963 and from where it managed to carry on working until April 1964. It returned to South Wales for scrapping at the Risca yard of Birds Commercial Motors. *BLP - W90.*

81XX No.8106 leaves Fladbury with a local freight for Worcester in March 1963. The 81XX was one of the smaller classes of the 2-6-2T type and were in fact 5ft 6in. rebuilds from 51XX engines reconstructed by Collett during 1938 and 1939. This engine was originally numbered 5120 prior to rebuilding and throughout the BR period it was allocated to Worcester shed from where it was withdrawn in November 1963. The ten strong class was widely distributed for most of its existence and in 1950 the breakdown was thus: 8100 - Leamington; 8101 - Kidderminster; 8102 - Neyland; 8103 - Oswestry; 8104 - Neath; 8105 - Bristol St Philips Marsh; 8106 - Worcester; 8107 - Neyland; 8108 - Tyseley; 8109 - Leamington. The first engine to be withdrawn was No.8105 in June 1957 and which was, by then, resident at Worcester. One of the class, No.8104, actually worked in Cornwall, at Truro shed, for a couple of months in mid-1956 but returned to Neath in the July. The last engine to be withdrawn was No.8109 from Tyseley in June 1965, it, along with 8104 was sold to private contractors for scrapping. The rest were dealt with at Swindon and none were preserved. Fladbury station closed in 1966 but the line between Worcester and Oxford is still open. *BLP - W104.*

'How the mighty....' This is 'Castle' No.5060 EARL OF BERKELEY working Up to London on the slow line with a heavy freight through Sonning cutting in May 1959. This engine had been allocated to Old Oak Common shed since February 1951 and although more commonly used for express passenger work it occasionally had to help out with the mundane goods traffic. More than likely, the Earl was due for a major overhaul and its time prior to a visit to Swindon would have been filled with jobs such as these. At its next general overhaul in the summer of 1961 it was fitted with a double chimney. Withdrawal came in April 1963 and No.5060 was stored at 81A for well over a year before departing for Swindon one last time in July 1964. It was scrapped at Cashmores yard in Newport. *BLP - W215.*

In June 1962, Keith Pirt caught Leamington based 41XX, No.4118, heading up Hatton bank bunker first with a Tyseley bound afternoon freight. Prior to transferring to Leamington in September 1954, this 2-6-2T had been allocated to Shrewsbury depot. Withdrawal took place in September 1962 and it stood derelict at Leamington shed for a year before purchase by J.Cashmore. It entered the Great Bridge yard in November 1963. *BLP - W282.*

56XX class No.6604 heads a long Up freight near Lapworth station on a cold November morning in 1961. The Tyseley based 0-6-2T still had plenty of life in it even at this late date. In September of 1962 it moved away to Croes Newydd where, at that time, there was still some useful employment for a locomotive such as this. No.6604 was condemned in October 1965 and was amongst the last of the class, a number of which were allocated to Croes Newydd. It was stored at Shrewsbury for a few weeks prior to making its last journey to Great Bridge. *BLP - W223.*

56XX No.5614 makes heavy going climbing through Hatton cutting with a Leamington-Tyseley freight in March 1962. This 0-6-2T was essentially a South Wales based engine but was captured on camera in the Midlands during its eleven months stay at Worcester shed from September 1961 until August 1962. During most of the 1950s it was allocated to Barry shed but on its return from Worcester it went to Abercynon where it was withdrawn a year later. *BLP - W243.*

Having spent much of it's BR career allocated to Oswestry shed, 32XX class 0-6-0 No.3200 had a late transfer to Templecombe shed on the Somerset & Dorset line in December 1963. That move probably gave it a further lease of life because it managed to stay operational until January 1965. After a period of storage at 83G it was towed to Swindon in April and cut up there shortly after arrival. This view, captured whilst No.3200 was still working the Cambrian lines, shows the engine climbing Llanbadarn bank with the morning local goods from Aberystwyth to Machynlleth in August 1963. *BLP - W56.*

Reading 'Castle' No.5067 ST FAGANS CASTLE climbs Hatton bank in fine style on a lovely autumn afternoon in October 1961 with a Birmingham bound express. Reading shed received this 4-6-0 during the previous May from Carmarthen and already they have given it a superb shine deserved of such a magnificent locomotive. However, the coming winter would be the last one in which it took part as an operational steam locomotive because it was condemned the following summer, one of fifty-five of the class withdrawn that year. After nearly two years stored at Swindon, No.5067 was sold to J.Cashmore in June 1964 and ended up at their Newport yard. *BLP - W6.*

One of the Worcester 'Castles', No.7031 CROMWELL'S CASTLE, pounds up Chipping Campden bank in March 1963 with a Worcester-Paddington express. Aided by an enthusiastic crew, who put on a fine show for the linesiders', this picture is one in a thousand. *BLP - W133.*

During a year when football specials were getting into the news for all sorts of fan misbehaviour, 'Castle' No.5007 ROUGEMONT CASTLE tackles the climb of Hatton bank in March 1962 with a Paddington to Villa Park football special. The writer has no idea of the outcome of the football match nor whether or not the coaching stock returned to London intact but the Gloucester Horton Road based 'Castle' was certainly only six months away from withdrawal. For much of it's BR life this engine was allocated to Cardiff Canton shed but moved to Old Oak Common in March 1957. Just under two years later it transferred to Swindon from where it worked for a further two years prior to moving to Gloucester. Horton Road only got eighteen months work from it before it was condemned. After a short two month period of storage at 85B it was purchased by Cashmores and ended up in their Newport yard by Christmas, one of thirty-seven 'Castles' cut up there. *BLP - W12.*

Old Oak Common 'Castle' No.7027 THORNBURY CASTLE speeds through Sonning cutting in May 1959 with a Cheltenham to Paddington express. In May 1960 this engine transferred to Worcester for a three year stay prior to moving onto Reading, its last depot, from where, in December 1963 it was withdrawn. In May of the following year it was purchased for scrap by Woodham's and moved in June to Barry docks. The 'Castle' languished there for eight years (one of the shorter residencies of that place) before being bought for preservation. *BLP - W129.*

So, Rowington troughs were still operational in September 1964 as demonstrated here by 'Castle' No.5091 CLEEVE ABBEY. The rather dirty Tyseley based 4-6-0 was in charge of a Down holiday extra returning to Wolverhampton. Just weeks away from withdrawal, No.5091 had moved to Birmingham during the previous June from Worcester, depot where it had spent about eight weeks after a six year stint in South Wales. This engine was one of the 'Star' class rebuilds which kept its original name after reconstruction but was renumbered from 4091. It was also one of the 'Castles' fitted with oil burning apparatus during that abortive scheme. Earlier BR allocations had seen it transfer from Swindon to Shrewsbury in May 1953 then, in September 1955, it moved to Chester for nearly two years. In June 1957 it spent the summer season helping out at Exeter prior to going off to Carmarthen at the start of its South Wales stint. It was condemned in October 1964 and sold straight away to Cashmores at Great Bridge. *BLP - W55.*

Another Reading 'Castle' No.4086 BUILTH CASTLE has steam to spare whilst working a Wolverhampton to Bournemouth train, composed of Southern Region stock, through Hatton cutting in October 1961. This was another of the class blessed with wanderlust during BR days. From Gloucester Horton Road it transferred to Carmarthen in October 1952 but only five months later moved down to Laira shed in Plymouth for four years. Swindon was its next abode from April 1957 until September 1959 when Reading got it for the first time which was until December when it then reallocated to Cardiff Canton for eighteen months. In May 1961 Reading got it back and No.4086 was withdrawn from there in April 1962. Yet another 'Castle' on the Cashmores shopping list, it entered their Newport yard in November 1962- hard to imagine when you look at this scene captured just one year previously. *BLP - W290.*

Crossing over the former Southern main line to Exeter (Central), 'Castle' No.5024 CAREW CASTLE heads westward out of Exeter (St David's) station on a sunny morning in May 1961 with an inter-regional working to Torbay. This engine spent much of it's BR career allocated to Newton Abbot depot from where it was withdrawn in May 1962. After a period of storage at Swindon works, it was sold to Cashmore's and cut up in their Newport yard. In the background is part of the former Great Western locomotive depot which, at this time, was still some way from its run down to closure for steam in October 1963. *BLP - W153.*

A very rural scene near Norton Bridge Halt, south of Worcester, in April 1963. The grubby 'Castle' is No.7002 DEVIZES CASTLE working a Worcester to Paddington express during the final full year of steam haulage of these trains. This was another 'Castle' equipped 'late in the day' (July 1961) with a double chimney. One could almost say that those fitted with a double chimney had an extended life but facts show that many of the single chimney engines lasted just as long in service as those so fitted. No.7002 was withdrawn in March 1964 at Worcester shed and ended up at Cashmores yard in Great Bridge by the summer. At least seventeen of the single chimney engines outlived No.7002. *BLP - W265.*

Dramatic though the picture may be, the engine is far from looking its best but it is September 1964 and 'Castle' No.7024 POWIS CASTLE was amongst the rapidly dwindling batch of the last of her kind. Having been allocated to Oxley shed for a year at this time (its appearance seems to confirm that fact), the 4-6-0 is speeding north over Rowington water troughs with a Down extra. No.7024 was one of the last of the dozen 'Castles' which survived into 1965 but it was not to be amongst those which carried on working through the year. Withdrawn in February 1965, it lay at Oxley shed until just after Easter when it was sold for scrap to Cashmores. It entered their Great Bridge yard in June and became one of the thirty-six engines from her class dismantled there. Allocated to Old Oak Common from new then Wolverhampton Stafford Road in August 1961, POWIS CASTLE was fitted with a double chimney in March 1959. *BLP - W203.*

'Modified Hall' No.7924 THORNYCROFT HALL heads for the west out of Exeter (St David's) in a graceful fashion with an evening passenger train in May 1961. The Taunton based 4-6-0 was one of the BR built engines of its class and when put into traffic in October 1950, was allocated to Westbury shed until November 1959 when Taunton got it. St Philips Marsh was its next home from January 1962 to May 1964 when it moved across Bristol to Barrow Road shed, which turned out to be the last stronghold of steam in the city. Withdrawal took place in December 1965 shortly after it was transferred to Oxford. Once again Cashmores had the purse out and No.7924 was towed to Newport. *BLP - W31.*

Two 'Castles' with a Down express on Rattery bank in July 1957 - magnificent but not unusual at that time. Nevertheless, it is still a sight to enjoy. Although the train engine was unrecorded by Keith, the leading engine is No.4075 CARDIFF CASTLE, a long time resident of Bath Road shed in Bristol. Unusually there is no reporting number displayed on the smokebox frame, perhaps there was little time for such niceties when No.4075 was attached at Newton Abbot. This double-heading would continue to Plymouth where CARDIFF CASTLE or perhaps both engines would detach in favour of a couple of 'Halls' or similar motive power for the onward journey of the train into Cornwall. Of all the 'Castles' illustrated in this album so far, No.4075 was the only one scrapped at Swindon. Withdrawn in November 1961, the by then Old Oak Common allocated engine was cut up in March 1962. *BLP - W219.*

Old Oak Common 'Hall' No.4919 DONNINGTON HALL arrives at Oxford in June 1962 and is passing the south crossing signal box as it enters the station in early morning sunshine with a Down excursion from Paddington. *BLP - W202.*

Reading based 'Hall' No.5957 HUTTON HALL threads Reading West cutting with a Down local train in May 1959. The azure sky and brilliant sunlight make for a superb picture. Having been allocated to Reading since 1950, No.5957 moved at the end of 1959 to Oxford, its last shed before withdrawal in July 1964. *BLP - W72.*

Laira based 'Hall' No.4967 SHIRENEWTON HALL leaves Truro tunnel with a Down stopping train for Penzance in June 1960. Diesel multiple units took over this service shortly afterwards. During BR days this engine spent about five years working from sheds in the West Country. It arrived at Newton Abbot in May 1956 ex Old Oak Common. A year later it transferred to Exeter for three months followed by a month at Penzance. In October 1957 it was back at 83A for a two-year stint this time after which it moved to Plymouth for almost eighteen months. In March 1961 Exeter shed got it for three months prior to it leaving for South Wales. It was withdrawn at Neath in September 1962, one of seventy-three 'Halls' condemned that year. *BLP - W195.*

One of the luckier 'Castles' was No.5080 DEFIANT, seen here speeding through Sonning cutting with a Swansea bound express in April 1962. Another former Canton top-link engine, No.5080 moved west to Landore in December 1955 then, in September 1956 went even farther west and ended up at Carmarthen for a five year residency. By the time this scene was captured, the 4-6-0 was allocated to Llanelly, its last depot from where it was withdrawn in April 1963. After languishing for nearly a year at Llanelly, DEFIANT was sold for scrap to a Woodham's at Barry and its removal to that place virtually ensured its future place in the annals of railway preservation. *BLP - W123.*

Cardiff Canton based 'Modified Hall' No.7913 LITTLE WYRLEY HALL pilots another unidentified 'Hall' on a Down express near Craven Arms in June 1962. *BLP - W187.*

In April 1960 'Hall' No.4974 TALGARTH HALL was photographed joining the Southern Region main line at Basingstoke with a special working off the Reading line. The 'Hall' had just been transferred from Tyseley to Stourbridge Junction so the train could have originated anywhere in the West Midlands. After spending most of the 1950s at Cardiff Canton shed, No.4974 left Wales via Pontypool Road in April 1958. The following November Tyseley got it. Gloucester Horton Road was its last depot, reached in September 1961. In the following April it was condemned and broken up at Swindon in September. *BLP - W238.*

During it's BR career, 'Castle' No.4081 WARWICK CASTLE had a somewhat interesting and varied allocation history. After spending nearly eight years at Landore depot in Swansea, it transferred to Canton in April 1958 but only for a few weeks because in June it was allocated to Exeter to help out with the seasonal holiday traffic heading for the West Country. In the following December Bristol Bath Road shed became its new home but only for six months when it went on loan to Shrewsbury. Back to Bristol in July, it stayed for another year and eleven months before reallocating to South Wales - this time to Llanelly - in June 1961. After a year there it went to Carmarthen for its last months of working during which time it was in charge of express passenger trains, London bound milk trains and goods traffic. Its demise occurred in the cold winter month of January 1963, one of forty-eight of the class struck off that year. Stored unserviceable until August, it was sold for scrap to R.S.Hayes of Bridgend. In this view No.4081 is setting out from Swindon with a Down express in March 1962. *BLP - W185*.

Talk about 'Bring a friend along to the party....' This is 63XX 2-6-0 No.6324 with, it is believed 22XX No.2206 passing through Swindon station in April 1962. Both locomotives are ex Reading shed, No.2206 is 'dead' having been withdrawn during the previous December. No.6324 is operational - just. Destination - the locomotive works. On arrival the 2-6-0 was condemned and cut up that month. The 0-6-0 was cut up in May. So, it can be confirmed that No.6324 was active to the very end. *BLP - W204.*

Croes Newydd based 28XX class No.2866 proceeds up Hatton bank towards Birmingham in October 1961. Having just undergone its final major overhaul at Wolverhampton's Stafford Road works, the 2-8-0 is returning light-engine to Wolverhampton after a running in turn, involving the haulage of a heavy Up freight, which had taken it to Banbury. Ten months after this scene was captured on film, No.2866 did in fact transfer to Banbury to run out its last months before withdrawal in March 1963. The engine was actually condemned at Oxford shed after reallocating there during that fateful month. After lying dormant at Oxford until Christmas 1963, No.2866 was hauled away for scrapping at Cashmores yard in Newport which was perhaps somewhat ironic because the big engine spent most of it's BR career working from sheds in South Wales including Newport's Ebbw Junction, Severn Tunnel Junction and Pontypool Road. *BLP - W4.*

Here is another early morning shot at Oxford but this time we go back to May 1959 as 'Grange' No.6821 LEATON GRANGE moves away from the station towards the shed under a superb clear sky. No.6821 was a newcomer to the Oxford (81F) allocation having arrived, via a repair at Swindon, from Laira in March. In November it was off to the west again but this time to Pontypool Road where it was resident, except for a three month loan to Ebbw Junction in summer 1961, until June 1963. St Philips Marsh was its next abode then onto the ex Midland shed at Barrow Road along with many other SPM orphans in June 1964. In October it moved to Llanelly but no sooner had it arrived and it was condemned. After a couple on months winter storage it was sold to Birds Commercial Motors at Bridgend, ready to feed the blast furnaces of Margam. *BLP - W246.*

Its work completed for the day, 4575 class No.5515 runs light through Par on its way to St Blazey shed on a June evening in 1960. This engine was allocated to St Blazey in August 1950 and after ten years working the various branches in the area, it was transferred to Taunton in November 1960. However, in February 1961 it was back in Cornwall, allocated this time to Penzance, for the coming summer season. That done it went to Plymouth Laira in September but was called into Swindon during November when it was condemned. Within a few months it had been purchased for scrap and was another exGWR locomotive which ended up in Cashmores scrapyard in Newport. *BLP - W208.*

'Manor' No.7800 TORQUAY MANOR, resplendent in BR lined green livery, backs into Barmouth station in August 1958 to take an Up express forward. This engine had just joined the Cambrian club, having transferred from Chester to Oswestry that same month. It was now to be a regular on the Cambrian lines and would often take its turn on the *CAMBRIAN COAST EXPRESS*. Which shed took time to clean the 4-6-0 - Machynlleth or it's home shed? Probably the latter started the process and the former finished it off. *BLP - W3.*

In 1960 only one large 'Prairie' was resident in Cornwall and that was St Blazey's 51XX class No.5198, seen here light engine rounding the curve at Par in June. The 2-6-2T was only allocated to 83E for the six months June to December having come initially from Gloucester Horton Road. Its end-of-year departure took it to Taunton shed from where it was withdrawn in June 1961. It was cut up at Swindon works during the following November. *BLP - W285.*

In the final weeks before its demise, 54XX class 0-6-0PT No.5410 works the Yeovil (Junction) to Yeovil (Town) auto-train in July 1963 with a pair of trailers. By now there were but three of this once twenty-five strong class of 0-6-0PT still in service and all were allocated to the former London & South Western shed at Yeovil Town [72C] (the former GWR engine shed at Pen Mill had closed its doors in January 1959). The class differed from the other eight hundred-odd Pannier tanks in having larger (5ft 2in) diameter wheels, being motor fitted and, from their introduction in 1931, they were intended to be used solely on passenger duties. Of the three which ended up at Yeovil, Nos.5410 and 5416 arrived in February 1963 from Westbury, to replace the Southern Region M7 class 0-4-4Ts, Nos.30052, and 30129, previously employed on the push-pull service. No.5420 arrived much later, in August, from Gloucester as a replacement for No.5416 which had been withdrawn that month. In September four of the smaller-wheeled but motor fitted 64XX class Panniers took over the remaining auto-train services around Yeovil. No.5410 went to Swindon works and was withdrawn in October. No.5420 returned to Barnwood shed in Gloucester and was also condemned - 54XX class was then extinct. None have been preserved. *BLP - W109.*

A far from immaculate 54XX No.5410 stands in the Southern Region station at Yeovil (Town) with an auto-train for the Junction station in May 1963. The same trailers illustrated in the previous view are in use again. *BLP - W234.*

In May 1961, auto-fitted 57XX Pannier No.9765, of Exeter shed, is pictured heading north out of Exeter with the Exe Valley auto-train bound for Dulverton on the Barnstaple-Taunton line. This service was more likely in the charge of the 14XX 0-4-2Ts with the 0-6-0PTs as first reserve. In latter years suitably equipped 4575 class 2-6-2Ts became frequent motive power. The former Great Western line to Dulverton had a dozen intermediate stations and halts including Stoke Canon on the main line prior to the junction. The train formation normally consisted two coaches with the locomotive leading out from Exeter. This Pannier tank had been at Exeter shed since April 1953, ex Laira. It was withdrawn in December 1961 and was an early purchase of scrap merchant J.Cashmore and ended its days in their Newport yard. *BLP - W29.*

Another Western Region engine standing in for withdrawn Southern engines was this very clean 57XX 0-6-0PT No.4666, seen in June 1960 passing Boscarne Junction with a Wadebridge to Bodmin (North) local train. This engine came to Wadebridge in December 1959, along with No.4694, from Danygraig via Exmouth Junction shed to take the place of SR O2 class 0-4-4T No.30236 which had been called into Eastleigh works and was withdrawn in January 1960. The other O2 at Wadebridge at that time, No.30200, worked alongside the 0-6-0PTs until it was transferred to Eastleigh in March 1961. Both of the Western Region engines were reallocated to Exmouth Junction in February 1963 and worked from that depot until withdrawn in June 1965. Later in the year they were sold for scrap to separate merchants in South Wales. *BLP - W239.*

In July 1963 'Manors' 7827 and 7828 undertook the Royal Train duties for which they had been cleaned so thoroughly at Machynlleth shed. In this view we see the pair with said train alongside the links at Aberdovey. *BLP - W34.*

(opposite) **During the BR period we were used to the 'Manors' being mainly associated with the Cambrian lines but they also worked in other areas of the country, including Devon and Cornwall. Here, in July 1957, No.7816 FRILSHAM MANOR runs through Bodmin Road station with a late afternoon Down freight. Even the engine's black livery has taken on a red tinge colour as the rays of the sun bathe everything in a warm glow. Note the original chimney is still carried. At this point in the 1950s most of the class were working in or near Wales but seven of them had homes in the West Country: 7816 was at St Blazey; 7809, 7812 and 7820 were at Laira; 7813 and 7814 were at Newton Abbot; 7823 at Penzance. St Blazey eventually had three of the class on its books at the same time but only for the three months June to September 1960 when they all left Cornwall. The last 'Manor' to leave the West Country was Newton Abbot's No.7821 which went to Croes Newydd in September 1961. Meanwhile, No.7816 got lined green livery (one of the last to do so) during a Heavy General repair at Swindon which commenced in April 1959 and probably included the fitting of a new narrower chimney. *BLP - W18.***

No.7810 DRAYCOTT MANOR, one of the original engines, departs Aberystwyth with that town's portion of the Up *CAMBRIAN COAST EXPRESS*, August 1963. *BLP - W21.*

(opposite) **Oswestry's No.7810 DRAYCOTT MANOR climbs Llanbadarn bank with the Aberystwyth portion of the Up *CCE* in July 1963. This engine spent its wartime (formative) years allocated to Banbury shed from where it, and the other four allocated 'Manors', worked to virtually all corners of the GWR system and sometimes beyond, especially Southern territory. In February 1947 it moved to Leamington then, in June 1948 to Stafford Road for three months before returning to Leamington. In December 1950 No.7810 transferred again but this time nearer to its eventual (spiritual?) home - Shrewsbury. This was the first 'Manor' to be allocated to Salop in the post-war period but it certainly was not to be the last. In December 1953 it moved to Gloucester Horton Road but was sub-shedded at Cheltenham for working both passenger and freight traffic on the MSWJ route to Southampton. In May 1959 DRAYCOTT MANOR finally got a foothold onto the Cambrian system when it was reallocated to Oswestry. In December 1963 it was transferred to Machynlleth, its final and perhaps its most appropriate move. However, times had changed and at the end of the Summer Timetable workings in September 1964, No.7810 was condemned. After laying derelict at Machynlleth it was hauled off to Swansea for scrapping in the first month of 1965.** *BLP - W136.*

'Manor' No.7819 HINTON MANOR departs Aberystwyth with the morning local to Machynlleth. This August 1964 view from the signal box shows the station before the alterations. *BLP - W175.*

By August 1964 all the 'Manors' were becoming somewhat grubby in appearance and No.7826 LONGWORTH MANOR was no exception. Here with an evening service to Carmarthen it is climbing the steep bank out of Aberystwyth. This was a long-time Carmarthen based engine (over ten years) but transferred to Llanelly in November 1963. Its last transfer was to Cardiff East Dock in February 1965, just two months before it was withdrawn. It was sold for scrap in the following summer. *BLP - W54*.

August 1963, No.7828 **ODNEY MANOR** at Aberystwyth shed, ex Royal train duty and now ready for the *CAMBRIAN COAST EXPRESS*. The BR Standard in the background contrasts nicely with the supershine finish. *BLP - W22*.

ODNEY MANOR again but in the July of 1963. This time waiting at Welshpool with a Shrewsbury to Aberystwyth train. The engine obviously has a good head of steam and appears to be impatiently expecting the whistle at any time. Withdrawn at Shrewsbury in October 1965, this was one of nine of the thirty strong class that passed into preservation. *BLP - W141.*

One year on and hardly looking its best in this one, 7828 ODNEY MANOR departs from Aberystwyth with an Up local in August 1964. *BLP - W221.*

Having paused to pick up passengers, 'King' No.6024 KING EDWARD I accelerates away from Teignmouth station with an Up express in July 1957. *BLP - W17.*

Here is the *CAMBRIAN COAST EXPRESS* at a different location, Hatton bank, with larger motive power in the shape of 'King' No.6019 KING HENRY V. The date is sometime in March 1962, a fateful year for the 'Kings' in which they were all withdrawn. However, KHV is giving no hint of being past it and is tackling the grade in fine style. No.6019 had just transferred from Cardiff Canton to Stafford Road shed where it joined ten other members of the class. One of those ten, No.6006, was already condemned and even as KHV was performing on Hatton, it lay in pieces at Swindon factory, the first to be cut up. After that things went from bad to worse for the class and in June seven of their number were condemned. No.6019's turn came in September when it was stopped at Old Oak Common shed and never worked again. Cashmores, Newport took it into their yard just before Christmas which coincided with the withdrawal of the last four engines - 6000, 6011, 6018 and 6025 - all of Old Oak Common. *BLP - W119.*

An unidentified but nevertheless immaculate 'King' departs from Dawlish station in July 1957 with the 7.15 a.m. Plymouth to Paddington express. On the Down line another passenger train leaves for the west. *BLP - W73.*

Giving off a superb wintry exhaust, 'King' No.6008 KING JAMES II passes Lapworth on an early morning express from Wolverhampton to Paddington in November 1961. For most of the 1950s No.6008 had been at Laira shed, having gone there from Stafford Road in July 1952. However, it returned to Wolverhampton in January 1959 and worked from 84A until withdrawn in June 1962. This was one of only ten 'Kings' which went back to its birthplace for scrapping. *BLP - W131.*

In contrast to the previous view, we present 'King' No.6011 KING JAMES I seen from the same lineside vantage point at Lapworth, hauling the same working but seven months later. This 'King' was recent acquisition for Old Oak Common, ex Stafford Road in September 1961. This engine worked to the end, being condemned at Swindon works in December. It was also one of those cut up at Swindon. *BLP - W214.*

This 4575 class 'Prairie' No.4587 was a Truro based engine in July 1957 when KRP caught it at Brent station, ex Newton Abbot works, after its last major overhaul. Looking resplendent in BR lined green, it has the larger version of the old emblem that always looked just too big when lining was applied. It had started it's BR career at Newton Abbot shed but moved onto Penzance in September 1953. It transferred to Truro in July 1954. Withdrawn in August 1960, it languished at Swindon works from September 1960 until April 1961 when it was finally broken up. *BLP - W226.*

Not since 1951, when it was allocated to Laira shed, would 'Hall' No.5968 CORY HALL have been a regular visitor to Exeter shed. However, on this day some ten years later in May 1961, the Shrewsbury based engine is coaled, watered and turned ready to return north with whatever working was given to it. What working brought it to Exeter in the first place? Perhaps we will never know. One thing for certain was that in October it transferred to Gloucester and in September 1962 it was condemned. After laying derelict at Horton Road engine shed for eighteen months, it was finally towed off to Newport where Cashmores yard welcomed it with open arms and in no time reduced it to a pile of scrap. *BLP - W261.*

A nice portrait of 'Hall' No.6940 DIDLINGTON HALL on the shed yard at Exeter in May 1961. The Newton Abbot based engine is turned ready to work westwards to Torbay or perhaps farther afield if traffic dictates. No.6940 had worked in the West Country on and off throughout the fifties. Transferring from Gloucester to Plymouth Laira in February 1951, it returned north eight months later to Stafford Road shed and after four months there moved to nearby Oxley. It was back in Plymouth by July 1952 and stayed for just over six years this time. 83A got it in November 1958 and kept hold of it for three and a half years before it moved away to Worcester for three months in June 1962. It was back to Gloucester then but only for a few weeks before Swindon shed required its services. Horton Road finally got it back in September 1963 and utilised it until May 1964 when it was condemned. No.6940 was another engine which ended up in the hands of Cashmores and was broken up at Great Bridge. *BLP - W167.*

43XX class No.5311 of Chester (GW) shed stands outside Barmouth station awaiting an Up train in April 1957. Pleasingly clean, the engine has the unlined green livery which suited the large emblem on the shallow sided tender. No.5311 started the 1950's decade working from Bath Road shed in Bristol and moved to Chester in April 1953. In December 1957 it returned to Bristol but went to St Philips Marsh instead. Six months later it transferred to Bath Road but reversed its course a year later and in April 1959 it was back at St Philips Marsh. This once large class of 342 locomotives had been whittled down to about 250 by Nationalisation and the withdrawals continued unabated throughout the 50s. No.5311's turn came in October 1960 but it was April 1961 before the Swindon cutting-up gang got to work on the engine. By 1964 all of the class had been withdrawn. Surprisingly only two of the class were preserved but one enterprising group of preservationists has since constructed an exact replica utilising parts from other ex GWR locomotives. *BLP - W68.*

Black liveried 51XX class 2-6-2T No.5183 departs from Newton Abbot with a midday local train for Kingswear on a glorious July day in 1957. This 'Prairie' tank was a relative newcomer to the Devon shed having arrived during the previous summer from Barry. At this time Newton Abbot shed could boast ten of the 51XX class on its books but many of them would be gone before the end of the decade, mainly for scrapping at Swindon. No.5183 was an exception in that it resided at 83A until April 1961 then it transferred to Wolverhampton Stafford Road where it managed a years employment before withdrawal. In total only twelve of the class were cut up by private contractors, the rest were dealt with at Swindon or, as in a few cases, Wolverhampton works. No.5183 went to Cashmores at Great Bridge in September 1962. Of course a couple managed preservation. *BLP - W92.*

July 1957. St Blazey based 45XX 2-6-2T No.4569 waits at Bodmin Road station with a close-coupled, non-gangwayed, compartmented brake composite 'B' set which formed the evening branch train to Bodmin (General). The first batch of 'B' set coaches, consisting of seven sets, was ordered from Swindon in 1922 and these were all in 'local' or branch line service by 1924. These particular vehicles had bodies that were 57ft long but thereafter the succeeding batches got longer until 61ft 2in. was reached about 1930. After this the GWR reverted to 57ft vehicles and that became standard up to the last coaches being produced in 1936. The two Diagram E145 coaches illustrated were built in the early 1930s, the first carriage being No.W6159W. Bodmin Road station has now been renamed Bodmin (Parkway) whilst the General station closed in 1967. The little Pannier transferred to Neyland in July 1961 but less than two years later it was back in England working from Westbury shed. It ended its day at Swindon shed, condemned there in July 1964. *BLP - W62.*

A delightful setting which conjures up thoughts of rural England in the summertime. It is a June day in 1960 and 45XX class No.4559 is heading a morning service of the Wadebridge to Bodmin Road local near Boscarne Junction. The small 'Prairie' had spent most of it's BR career allocated to St Blazey depot and would be condemned there during the October following the capture of this scene. After residing at Swindon works for a couple of months in early 1961, it was purchased by Woodham's and entered the Barry yard during that summer, however, it was not one of the lucky ones and was broken up almost immediately. *BLP - W207.*

The branch line from Truro to Falmouth is still in use today although scenes such as this one at Falmouth are but a memory. However, in June 1960 the branch train from Falmouth terminus to Truro consisted this 'B' set and a Gangwayed Brake [BG] (to be attached to an eastbound train on the main line) coupled to the motive power - a Collett 4575 class 2-6-2T, No.5552 of Truro depot. This engine had, at the time of this photograph, less than four months operational life in front of it and was withdrawn in October. It ended up, by January 1961, at Woodhams yard in Barry and languished there for twenty-five years before being taken away for preservation in June 1986. Built in 1928, it was the 174th steam locomotive to be rescued from Barry and is one of ten of its class to be preserved. No.5552 now runs, appropriately, in Cornwall, on the Bodmin & Wenford Railway, doing what it was built for in the first place - to run the branch lines. *BLP - W79.*

The 41XX class 2-6-2T had the same size coupled wheels as the 61XX engines, 5ft 8in., but the boiler pressure was somewhat less at 200 lbs. p.s.i. as against 225 lbs. On a late June afternoon in 1962, Leamington based 41XX No.4125, wearing the lined green livery, and hauling a 20-ton brakevan, makes its leisurely way towards Banbury along the main line through Kings Sutton - the day's work nearly completed. A long time resident at Birkenhead shed, this 'Prairie' came south to the Midlands in March 1957 and stayed until withdrawal in June 1965. During that time it was allocated at various times to Tyseley, Oxford and of course Leamington. This class was equally at home hauling freight, local passenger trains and semi-fast traffic. No.4125 was sold for scrap to a contractor in South Wales. *BLP - W191.*

Not quite looking its best but nevertheless coping easily with this Basingstoke to Reading local train, 61XX class large 'Prairie' No.6138 of Oxford shed gets its three-coach train on the move away from Basingstoke in March 1960. One of the earlier withdrawals within this class, No.6138 had spent most of it's BR career at Oxford but ended up at Reading shed in July 1962 to work out its last year. Condemned in August 1963, it entered Swindon works and was cut up there in November. *BLP - W205.*

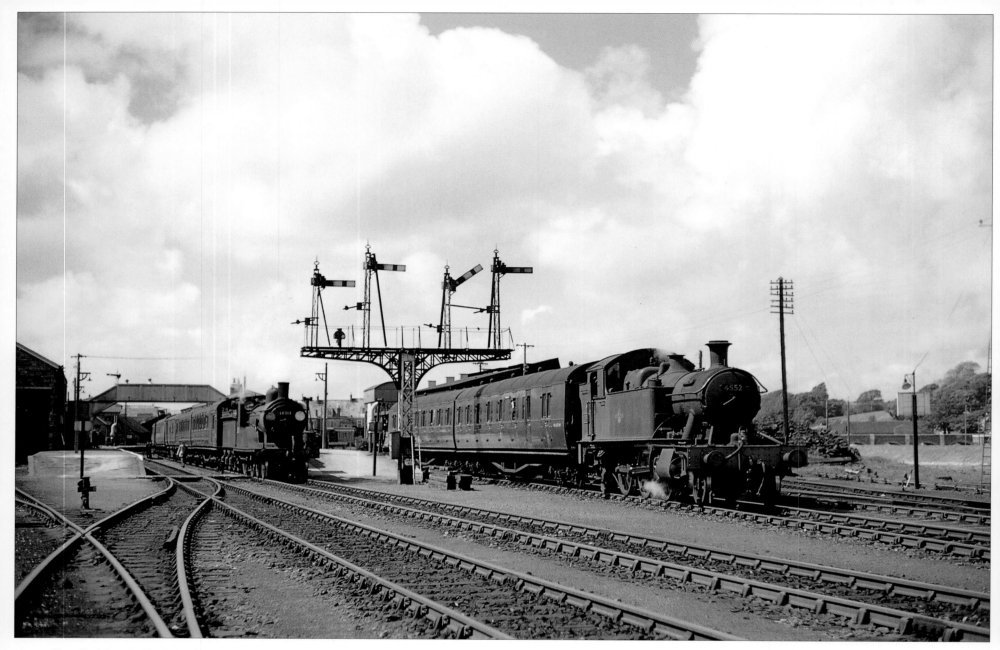

Signalled for the Bodmin line, 45XX class No.4552 departs from Wadebridge with a stopping train in June 1960. In the station a Southern Region T9, Exmouth Junction based No.30313, is awaiting its departure time with a service to Exeter. The former LSWR shed at Wadebridge housed, by now, nothing larger than the three ancient Beattie 0298 class 2-4-0WT engines (30585, 30586 and 30587) used on the Wenford Bridge mineral line and resident at Wadebridge for some sixty-odd years. Alongside them were solitary Class O2 No.30200 and the pair of 57XX PTs mentioned elsewhere in this album. Of course, when the engine shed here came under Western Region control it was 'all change' and the Beattie Well tanks were withdrawn in December 1962, their replacements, a trio of WR 1366 class 0-6-0PTs having arrived during the previous summer. What of the 2-6-2T No.4552? It had been a long time resident of St Blazey shed and would remain so until withdrawn in September 1961 at Wolverhampton works where it was cut up. *BLP - W216.*

Waiting in Par station with a local train for the Newquay branch in June 1960, 4575 class No.5557 sports the unlined green livery which was starting to become very popular then with BR accountants. The side tank does, however, show the new BR emblem. How many of you remember changing here from the main line to the waiting branch train? This was the 2-6-2Ts last summer and at the end of the timetable period the little 'Prairie' travelled to Swindon where it was condemned in October. Later on it was sold to Woodhams at Barry and stood derelict in the sidings there until it was cut up at some time after 1965. *BLP - W230.*

2251 class No.2232 departs Portmadoc with a late afternoon local train to Pwllheli in August 1958. On arrival the Machynlleth based 0-6-0 would be able to take advantage of the new locomotive servicing facilities recently opened by British Railways at Pwllheli. After turning, watering and perhaps taking a little coal on board, it would await the evening service that would take it back home rather than stay overnight in the new two road engine shed. No.2232 was another 0-6-0 that spent much of it's BR career on or near the former Cambrian lines. Variously allocated to Croes Newydd, Shrewsbury, Stourbridge Junction and Machynlleth, it broke away from it's Welsh connections in February 1961 and transferred to Bristol St Philips Marsh. A year later it moved to Horton Road, Gloucester and finally, in March 1963 to Worcester from where it was withdrawn in September 1964. It was purchased for scrap by Cashmores and could have easily gone to their Newport yard but instead went to their Great Bridge yard where the Welsh connection was severed for ever. *BLP - W66.*